Why I Was Late

Why I Was Late

Charlie Petch

Brick Books

Library and Archives Canada Cataloguing in Publication

Title: Why I was late / Charlie Petch.
Names: Petch, Charlie, author.
Description: Poems.
Identifiers: Canadiana (print) 20210224592 | Canadiana (ebook)
20210224630 | ISBN 9781771315579 (softcover) |
ISBN 9781771315586 (HTML) | ISBN 9781771315593 (PDF)
Classification: LCC PS8631.E7975 W59 2021 | DDC C811/.6—dc23

Though much of the work of Brick Books takes place on the ancestral
lands of the Anishinaabeg, Haudenosaunee, Huron-Wendat, and
Mississaugas of the Credit peoples, our editors, authors, and readers
from many backgrounds are situated from coast to coast to coast in
Canada on the traditional and unceded territories of over six hundred
nations who have cared for Turtle Island from time immemorial. While
living and working on these lands, we are committed to hearing and
returning the rightful imaginative space to the poetries, songs, and
stories that have been untold, under-told, wrongly told, and suppressed
through colonization.

We at Brick Books gratefully acknowledge the Canada Council for the
Arts, the Government of Canada through the Canada Book Fund, and the
Ontario Arts Council for their support of our publishing program.

Conseil des arts Canada Council
du Canada   for the Arts

Canada

ONTARIO ARTS COUNCIL
CONSEIL DES ARTS DE L'ONTARIO
an Ontario government agency
un organisme du gouvernement de l'Ontario

BRICK BOOKS

Brick Books
487 King St. W.
Kingston, ON
K7L 2X7
www.brickbooks.ca

In loving memory of sweet Zoëdog

Table of Contents

I

II

III

IV

V

VI

I

Dear C-3PO

*To be accompanied by a ukulele & musical saw
loop-pedal build, done to the tune of "Can't Take My
Eyes Off You" by Bob Crewe & Bob Gaudio.*

I always thought you were gay
I imagined there was a
little glorious hole
somewhere in R2-D2
and when you made love
he made those happy
  hrrr hrrr brwing tup
  whrrr hrr
sounds

Maybe he would turn his head
all around to see you
try to read joy
in your manufactured face

I always thought you a top
that R2-D2 hummed love songs
that didn't sound preprogrammed
or desperate
or othering

C-3PO
was your golden exterior
made up of melted-down wedding rings
tossed into vats at the training schools
the sheddings of those
ready to die?

These galaxy warriors
who laughed at what made you feminine
which sounds like hesitation
which sounds like
we are afraid
to feel

How you must have keened
every time your lover
went to war
became a plug in another machine
(as unprotected as a jet wing)

Your gold-plated face
never told us
that behind the joke
was a man in love
with a soldier

I felt your tears my sweet
though your face
betrayed
nothing

My First Boyfriend

Years before you killed someone

you pulled my drunk friend
out of the water
breathed mist on a dock
I handed you my sweater
watched you pull your shirt over your head
lights lapping at lake water   chest

Years before you killed someone

your mouth full of shy
you gave me a beaded bracelet
that was so mismatched
I knew your sister didn't help

Years before you killed someone

we were barefoot
callused with summer
you held sumac to my face
inhaled its iced tea fragrance

Years before you killed someone

I sat in your room
tortured Ethel the action figure
until your little brother came in

mocked you for playing with "girl stuff"
and I laughed at you too

Years before you killed someone

I listened to kids who told me
you were a loser
friends I never had before
ones I secretly wanted
I cracked your twelve-year-old heart
put the bracelet into your hand
the one I used to hold

Years later your parents left too
sent you to military school
not everyone can raise the children they get
I went to your birthday party
ended up hiding in a washroom
for fear of military boys
who grab at breasts
impress with ammo talk
hold women like weaponry

You were lost to be found
accepted payment to kill a stranger
his wife enticing with sumac breath
a chance to be bully
you bragged about it to a girl
who was so impressed she called the cops

Before you killed that man
maybe the world felt like prison
every escape attempt
another clanging door
girls' laughter like lockdown

I remember the boy you might have been
stepping carefully past sumac
Did you know it was poison then
that enemies smell sweetest
that betrayal is a part of growing up
that my first boyfriend
started off heroic?

Broiled Meat

When I think of
animals being roasted
they are never headless

Mouths broiled in scream
lit by a greasy oven light
or turning over an oil drum
smoke rising as eyes evaporate
vitreous escape into steam

Yesterday I donated
my body to science
Should they reject me
it will be my sad second death

They may still take my eyes
for transplant
I used to be
a hospital bed allocator
My job was to get bodies
in and out of the hospital
alive   or dead   or organ
Patients' eyes would sit
on my desk floating in fluid

I don't fear death
or turn away
Its eyes follow me
everywhere

When I was certain
the man who picked me up
hitchhiking would kill me
I cracked open a beer
realizing how little I could do
and relaxed in a way
my whole life had prepared me for

My mouth agape
my eyes already leaving
my body ready for science

Schoolyard Theatre

Concrete with tufts of grass
iron gates
sharp corner into chain-link
We would flatten ourselves
against it
and wait for the Great Director
Maria Manoulo
to arrive

I had avoided recess for a few years
(no one asks the volunteers
what they're hiding from)
but the new librarian
needed no help

Forced to trade
the sanctuary of books
for the unending rehearsal
of Maria's script
I could not have been happier

Every lunch period the same scene
        (Lights fade up on a tired rec room
        TEENAGERS are having a party
        MOTHER comes home drunk
        DAUGHTER is caught drunk
        with BOYS in the house
        who are also drunk)

Maria always cast herself as Drunk Mom
The others clamoured
for the part of the daughter
while I revelled
in being the boy

You see
in the moments before
Drunk Mom came home
I had girlfriends
beautiful girlfriends
I wooed   I witted   I winked

They called me Charlie
or Mike or Tom
giggled when I slung arm onto shoulder
put hair behind ear
sometimes we'd neck
by rubbing our necks together

These moments of male
started the slow feeling
that my skin was drag
that if I was tomboy enough
I could flat-chest hide forever

But Drunk Mom
would come home
bust up the party
order Mike
or Tom or Charlie home

then fall down
into a giggling
gaggle
of girls

But oh how delicious life was
when I was a guy at a party
fake smoke and drink in hand
my body relaxed
into boy
my swagger saved
for schoolyard theatre
where I finally
didn't
have to
act

Stealing Candy at the Movies

You always stole the candy
we'd eat during the library's "Thursday Thrillers"
but never spoke of where they took your mother

Banana Marshmallows for *The Man with the X-ray Eyes*
Candy Corn for *Nosferatu*
Swedish Berries for *Invasion of the Body Snatchers*

Though our Catholic school said stealing was a sin
I always felt you were owed more in this life
and never questioned your thefts
just like how we never questioned why the library
showed these movies to ten year olds

As we got older and candy turned into glue bags
you'd never share with me
and scary movies always failed in comparison
to your life

I watched the boy I loved
morph into a lost skinhead
who ran faster than nightmares

and always into
the arms of a family
any family
that would have you

The Ballad of Owen Hart

To be performed with a loop-pedal build on
dulcimer and viola.

Wrestling died on live TV
My brother and I
saw the cameras sway
saw them fight not to look
at your fallen beauty

Son of Stu
brother of Jim, of Davey, of Bret
cousin of Rowdy Roddy Piper
your family trained generations
of gentleman and lady wrestlers

But that all changed
May 23rd, 1999
when Owen
you walked up ninety-nine steps
got strapped into an untested harness
and were thrown to your death
in the ring

Owen
as you free-fell thirty metres
what thoughts were with you

as the clip failed to catch
as the crowd cheered your names

BLUE BLAZER

who said he could fly
or

OWEN HART

who trusted he would

Maybe
as you rushed towards death
you touched the small
razor blade in your pants
worried you'd land on it

Maybe
you said God's name

Maybe
you thought the mat
would bounce your body back

Did you curse Vince McMahon
who turned your father's legacy
into the mechanism
of your death

Blue Blazer
that morning
you kissed
your bed-headed children goodbye
liplocked your wife
promised her
you weren't going to do the stunt

How did you get
from Martha's relieved embrace
to falling to your death
on
      LIIIVE PAY PER VIEW?

Was it because you knew
that pure wrestling
has no hero's reward?
That pride and tradition
won't put food on the table?
That the Olympics only come
every four years?
But the wrestling franchise
is on
      EVERY NIGHT OF THE WEEK

and to win
you cannot be Owen Hart
who saves every dime for his family
who comes from Canadian royalty

You have to put on costumes
that make you feel foolish
You have to be The Blue Blazer

YOU HAVE TO FLY

When kids wrestle now
they use shattered fluorescent tubes
folding tables
metal chairs
and ladders
that lead nowhere

In the Distance

In the distance
a train
In the foreground
dusty boys
The leader places
a penny on the rails

It will be fifteen days
before his mother
steps onto the tracks

He will imagine
her waist
pulverized copper

The most quieted of them
places a quarter
he stole from beneath
his sister's pillow
still elated at the way
this made her crumble

The last boy
grins at the gold ring
It belongs to the uncle
who feeds him booze
before he fucks him
The boy
waits for the train
It will be so loud
he will be able to shriek
finally

They have been told to be boys
They have been told to be men
There is no crying here
no words of wisdom
between friends
All that is unsaid
tastes of metal
sits on the rails
waits to be
forced into shapes
and bragged about

Things You Didn't Know about Me

To be performed with dulcimer.

When I was five I put flags
on all the anthills on our driveway
because I had no other friends to save

I used to ghostwrite a blog
for male enhancement products
I'd have sex with my fictional girlfriend
and write reviews of the performance

I let gibberish happen
when alone
to relieve myself
of disability

Ever since I got a strap-on
I've really been able
to maintain an erection

While working as a best boy
I opened a drawer labelled
"Just Legs"
 at a morgue

I've always wanted
a gay grandfather
but this doesn't mean
I never wished to be alive

I constantly strive to outlive my dog

I once hitchhiked with
sports exposé novelist
and shunned knuckleballer
Jim Bouton
the creator of Big League Chew

II

Wookie Love

To be accompanied by a "A Place to Sleep," a tango recorded with The Silver Hearts during my tenure with the band.

Chewbacca
you are my favourite
of all of the wookies

since I saw you in the first movie
which is actually the fourth movie
you have ruined me for all of humanity

Chewie

there is never enough chest hair to satisfy me
never enough back hair to warm the cockles of my
star-warring heart
the smell of sweat and hair is not husky musky enough
to fully fill my
little tusk

But I try I try
    Just back from the gym?
    Bring that hairy ass in

The love cries of my partners have never equalled
the parallel universe of what comes out of your
        small-toothed mouth
Why are you not more sabre-toothed?
Light sabre-toothed platitudes of love from you would
        be like
sweet baths of sound
guttural bubblings
of glorious ghastly sex

Would you make me wear a mohair onesie
so that you could accept me as your own?
Would you have me stop manscaping my landscape
so that there'd be somewhere soft for you to land?

Chewbacca   would you only chew my bacca
if the hair was long enough to be tangled with yours?

I want to twist and turn and grind you until we become
dreadlocked
        (I'd take them out later though   because I'm white)
I want my skin to be patterned in scraped lines
of the lineage you left to be with me
for our kitchen to smell of victory sage
and the rubbed salts of galaxy seas

We could live our lives
as naked apes
        (although I would still wear a sports bro or binder
        because it really feels weird not to have one on)

Maybe we could both wear sports bros or binders
and dance to space music created for us
by the human John Williams

I didn't think our love
could outlast my crush on
Han Solo
but when I'm with my
han(d)s solo
it is your Wookie cry
that blushes my neck
your feet (that must smell of freedom)
I want resting in the backs of my calves

It is you Wookie man
your ammo belt
crashed to my floor
your tendrils caught in my
over-flossed teeth
that pull out my belief
that the language we seek
need never include the
oppressive learning of English

Wookie I cry out
    WAAHHARRRHHH
in hopes someday, you might cruise
your Millennium Falcon my way

Church & Gerrard

*To be performed with ukulele, musical saw, a jar
of fake bacon bits, metal tongs, & a serrated knife
on loop pedal to the tune of "Running to Stand
Still" by U2.*

What happens at 5 a.m.?
Mansor   my boss
falls asleep in his van again
there's no cell phone to be had
and the sky is blinking blue
and the knife I keep hidden
comes out of my shoe

Mansor's taught me many things
about late-night hot dog vending
Cut the wieners diagonal in the front
then a long line in the back
they lie flat

Keep the onions frying in grease
that smell is the best kind of tease
But he hasn't told me what to do
when I'm the last one on the street

The sex workers are nowhere to be found
they've stopped calling out
  hot dog girl
cause they just like the sound
stopped ordering sausages from back seats of cars
stopped enduring the yelling of men spilling from bars

The pimps are all gone too
they're not here to tell me that
I should hook too

that I could
  go to Hawaii
and if I
  get knocked up
they can
  clean out inside
me

Don't I
  want better money than this?
Don't I want to
  start each evening with a kiss?

And I think if I do that I'll just end up with a hula girl
charm on my wrist
that I'll lie back and watch her sway
as I get fucked but never kissed

It's been hours since drunken questions
I almost miss the slurred inflections
Yes I sell things that look like dicks
No I just turn sausages not tricks
Sorry I don't have any corn relish
and the bacon bits aren't real
and I'm barely staying awake
because hot dogs are my only meal

It's 5 a.m. now and I'm falling asleep
with hundreds of dollars shoved under my feet
If only I'd left with that sweet sweet dyke
who said she'd double me home on her bike
Maybe she'd be surrounding me with sex like art
making me believe that I am too smart
to fall asleep behind this goddamned hot dog cart

The sun splatters onto the street
as I breathe in fumes of propane and day-old meat
and somewhere else   Mansor   you snore in your van
and somewhere else I nod off again

Dropping Doves

To be performed while playing " Over the Rainbow,"
written by Yip Harburg, on the musical saw.

He was the abusive alcoholic father I never had
    Fucking her was like parking a school bus in an
    airport hangar
he'd say to their son   the best boy
who was only called that
when he was on his dad's lighting crew

Five years I worked for those two

unloaded trucks, ran cable, mounted lights
got asked for so many blow jobs I finally told his son
    Whip it out get it hard I won't touch it with anything
    but my lips

Five years I stayed with the crew everyone hated
because there was always another movie
because I like the feel of drowning
because I want to be feared

The show that made me leave them started like this
    All right guys we have another movie
    It's about some fag that got killed
    It's called The Matthew Shepard Story

Matthew
it felt like your ghost drifted into
our truck full of carny leers
and Ferris wheel parts
reminding me

being a man doesn't mean
you have to bellow like a ringmaster
hoist an elephant onto a caravan
or corner me with stories of gang rape
as I helplessly get turned on

Some men seem as brittle as magicians' doves
raise their voices only in joy
but they are so strong

Matthew how did you
forgive the beasts who bashed you
who left you tied to a farmer's fence
singing mourning songs for days?

We met your mom
told your story
As our queer community filled the ring
cruel jokes dropped like doves meeting glass
and I finally started moving towards
better models of masculinity

Matthew
we like such brutal men
because life can be terrifying
and bullies
look just
like
bodyguards

I stayed for one last show

I didn't want to leave you
alone with them
Matthew

Waltzing Armageddon

How they danced

when they knew the bomb was coming
how easily hands found elbows
how hips shared rhythm
and quivering lips shaped music

The announcement came
a declaration
of Armageddon
and they waltzed into the streets

Some were the rehearsed dances of marriage
others learned on the feet of fathers
or were created in darkened living rooms
or called out in brightly-lit barns

Heads hit shoulders
dropping like meteors
the inevitability of the universe
the sanity of counted steps
Flashes came
skin turned to dust
lover's lips
grafted in goodbyes

their whispered songs
rippling waves of wishes
sailing the death of them
into the xenon-bright night sky

and we drive into this
an alien convoy
of their dump trucks
rolling over hips   heads
hands fused to
the smalls of backs
ready to dispose
of human grace

Life Is Easier When I'm a Misogynist

Life is easier when I'm a misogynist
I get the jokes
make the jokes
am the jokes

I grew up "tomboy"
climbed and leaped and played war games
tried to learn how to fight
without kicking balls
wished so hard my name was Charlie
that I turned my back on my sisters

I so wanted to be feared
I scared myself

I worked with my body
left my mind at home
where it grew increasingly
uncomfortable
with the violent acts
made by my mouth

but they don't hire you back
when you're feminist

I started off mornings unpacking trucks
or stocking bars or building stages
revelled in male spaces
wore tool belts
dragged my drag along
tied to the dead weight
of a girl's misfortune

It is still in me
to show how I can never be offended
this bystander effect
of an affected speech pattern
this need to be "one of the guys"

It's so much easier isn't it
to cloak yourself in a history
where speaking about oppression
is just something that holds you back
where you can be the hero
the most hilarious
be the bro

I try to be a better person
see how rape culture is my culture
look at my words differently
educate myself so that you
don't have to

No longer do I
flex daredevil
trade my sisters
for a bro code
or wake up next to someone
who didn't deserve
all I so freely gave them

My fellow man
and those who hide in full view
it is never too late for this change
for power to be a genderless exercise
Those who love you
will be relieved
those who won't
just aren't ready to give up
their stronghold on fear

Because look
I'm still one of the guys
they're just better guys

Eat Prey Love

To be performed with an insect voice & stance.

Victor

six hours of straight lovemaking is a lot

While I recognize
our species of praying mantis
needs to propagate
I just got really tired and hungry

I appreciate you brought us
soft-bellied flies to dine on
and even a cricket
to play a back-leg tune
until we ate that too

Maybe it's a bit old fashioned
to expect you to provide the food
to have punished you
for my empty digestive tract
but let's face it
I was always going to be a single mom

My own mother taught me many things

like decapitating your partner during copulation
helps them to ejaculate

like that us praying mantis
don't actually have to pray
like death is a part of life
like love doesn't last
unless it is

broken down by enzymes
in the midgut
digested into protein
and passed along
to the next generation

I'm told
your son has
your eyes
your beady black eyes
but I had them first
then I had the rest of your head
and your delicious thorax

I'm so sorry Victor but

six hours
is a long time
for a quickie

Electric

Having touched the back
of a bare wire neon sign
you flew
woke
in a graceless clump
and went right back to work

Film punks with power
we carried ourselves
larger than lightning
hoped waterproofing worked
prayed no inspector
would check for safety

Who needs a harness when you have
an eight ball in your brain?
A truck full of fuck you're tough?
A bare-knuckle apartment
windowsills of booze
and supine mirrors
too dusty to reveal the
collage of scars
that used to look like you

The union sells our sleep
the producer no longer looks
at us hard enough
to tell the insurance
what could have prevented this
terrible accident

The world is our film set
Somehow we have power over power
park trucks   spiderweb cable lines
guess at regulation
thinking that three hours of sleep
can fuel your eighteen-hour day

Fuck a truck your balls shoot nails
you hit the rails in front of you
no one expects you to be human

Your family left the zombie
that ate your brain
fuck them fuck that bitch
Now we just stay on TV
live your life in film trucks fuck...

fuck this life
that took your kids
Kids that watch you sleep at the zoo
yell when the car pulls to the shoulder
or dreams into oncoming traffic

When the film wraps
when the truck parts are rolled out
counted
shoved back into buildings full of men
who know our names
but not our names

for once   you get enough sleep

Upon waking, turn on
the show to catch the credits
Laugh at the names of our union family
the only ones we have
patience for anymore

For a second before passing out
there's a sensation
that you used to be someone else
before the union bartered us
shortened our lives

Turn off the television
see yourself reflected
A hollow man trapped
in a blank glass headstone

Why I Was Late

I could not find the right
theme music
and there is a wormhole
where my front door used to be

My dog thinks I'm dead
whenever I leave
Could you do that to her
everyday?

I'm too busy remembering
what I try to forget
I sewed my only watch
inside of me
I'm waiting for the world
to be ready

Someone took my body
and when they were done
they handed it back to me
neatly folded
and said
      Keep this in a safe place
and now I can't find it

I've changed the locks
so many times
I don't trust myself
not to bring home
the next reason

56

III

Buried Treasure

*If you are currently eating, I'd recommend you
stop until you're done this poem. To be performed
with sexy dulcimer.*

For a second I glance
at that spot
by your blushing earlobe
my treasure glinting

I force my attention
back
don't let on
don't stare

Will my mouth
travel down your chest?
Suck your nipples hot
blow them cold
linger at arched pelvis
and then tongue you like a
weathered stallion at a salt lick?

Will I taste us
before I ask
with cum-tangy breath
for you to
   turn over

You gaze at my fetish-glazed eyes
fear fluttering flaccid state

Why?
you ask
my attempts at being casual
laughable

You um... have
some bacne you can't get to
let me help you

You turn over
and the poetry of your blemishes
open soft-cover sweetly

There it is

a story of trapped dirt, oil
and capped
worms buried in pores
a revolution
waiting to be freed
by my trim fingertips

When you're not around
I think about those three aged blackheads
by your ear
imagine long lingering dunking baths
heated lavender cloths
ambient music playing
trip hop tales of our
estheticia

Oh, do not think I'm the only one
We find each other at garden parties
strawberry socials
and at the bottom of wine bottles

Loosened by liquor
we speak freely
of acne vulgaris
closed comedones
open comedones
papules
and refilling papulopustulars

We are at your spas
We're staring at the back of your sweaty neck right now
We go to school for twenty years to call ourselves
dermatologists
but we are lovers
freedom fighters

We can identify our lovers' bodies
by the scars that we leave
      Yes officer, it's them, I'm sure of it
we'll say with tears brimming
knowing we can never press
those pores again

Let us heal you
Don't make us live in shame
our passions spent downloading
"Biggest Zit Pop Ever"
"Cysts of Cyprus"
"Infected Boils of Istanbul"

And so dear reader
when you finally relent
and let me at your back
know that the nugget
I extract and then present to you
with all the affection of a
murderous cat
is me showing you

the pus
real love
is made of

Crave

Sulfur meeting cigarette end
gasoline pumps
steaming Buick leather interiors

my first memories of smell

My nose is not for fresh-cut flowers
it craves the sharp
the fume
the clouds that seep
through hands held over mouths

odours that
congeal into savoury spit
the dung of horses
taste of gallivant
my dog's feet
tang of freedom
weeping ulcers
descend my drool

I breathe easy in emergency rooms
snort side-of-the-highway car wrecks
joy wells in my eyes
as dynamite demolishes

My nose is man-made
My sinus cavities are cities
My dreams drip down coal mines
My olfactories are old factories

You used to talk about living in the country
and I would fill our lot with auto skeletons
wish your hands oil-stained pungent

You smell different
now that I fear you

My First Lisping Hero

To be performed with ukulele fingerpicking.

We called you champ

Mike Tyson

when you and I open up our mouths
they turn into bull's eyes
and we are silent in our defense
because words can be land mines

The first time I saw you
unabashed unapologetic on the
microphone

you became my lisping hero

I imagined us in my playground
bullies fleeing our earthquake footsteps

I tried to duck and dance like a butterfly Ali
You were no one's punching bag
launched iron fists to the tune of thirty-eight arrests
before you hit age thirteen

The boxing world plucked you from reform school
maybe you felt saved
I know how education can seem like the enemy
and for a boy targeted for his
high-pitched lispy voice
you probably felt relieved that the teacher
would never call on you again

Your lisp never got better
your voice never dropped
you put up your dukes
gave up on language
and let your dreams narrow

Before your mom died
she gave you to
your boxing coach
Cus D'Amato
who polished you up like a
custom auto
but never could install any brakes

There were no bells in the bedrooms you strode into
no towels to be thrown in front of your thundering ways

Raised to be a wild animal
you look calmest wrestling with your Bengal tiger
even your friends said you belonged in a cage

But Mike
you're as used to betrayal as getting punched in the gut
I mean the man who could have protected you
left
when you were just two years old

There are no s sounds in "Dad"
you could have said it every day
without the worry of retribution

Instead you shouted it into barrel chests
It bounced back with the blank stares of men
who loved you
for your fists
and the bags of money they bring

Maybe what you needed
was a male embrace
not cut short by a bell

Now in the wake of Holyfield's spat-out ear
your empire crumbles
your four-year-old daughter dies
your other children look at you in fear
and your beloved tiger
paces behind some stranger's bars

The television calls you a monster
speaks of your failures
your crimes
your legacy of violence

Mike
I like your new heavyweight fight
the one called Sobriety
as your daughter's easy laughter
makes you champion
the father who's there
the father who came back

I've written so many endings
to your poem   Mike
some were too kind
others damned you
but you grew
in love and recovery

Some humans are capable of so much
when we give them a chance
to get up off the mat

Ashes to Ashes

The priest would smear ashes
on my forehead
with his thumb

I wondered if they were
burnt bits of parishioners
Is that what made them authentic?

But the body was unleavened bread
the blood was cheap red wine
nothing was as advertised

Tom and I would
ash into our hands
sometimes pot
sometimes hash
sometimes tobacco

Ashes to ashes
dust to dust

Ashing our foreheads
was just our thing
We never told the other guys

because one of us knew
what it was like
to be touched by a priest

and one of us knew
how to accept that our body
could also be cheap booze

and both of us knew
what it was like
to have bull's eyes
smeared onto our foreheads
and be force-fed the silence
that scripture requires

Throw Yourself on Furniture

Your favourite
sausage gravy and biscuits
Every birthday I spent
finding Jimmy Dean filling
tried not to think
about your arteries

Now
after watching you
have a heart attack
rising dough
smells of antiseptic
fried fat
tastes of hospital mops

The oven timer
reminds me of your cries
when the painkillers wore off
clamped for an angiogram
screams of captivity

There are plans today
nieces   nephews
sister and brothers-in-law
a beloved road trip
I hope will erase this meal

but you tell me
with focussed frown
that all you want for your birthday
is for me to be gone

My throat shrinks vein-sized
as I push Jimmy Dean sausage down it
say I understand

What they don't tell you
about heart attacks
is that sometimes
there is brain damage

that your husband
could come home
a stranger

When I was fourteen
I choked on a metal
pop-can tab
while alone
impaled myself
abdomen to chair back
until the shiny bloody disk
flew to table top

As my throat closes
around your obstruction
and I'm not sure if I'm to choke
or if it's silent sobs
I wonder if
I'll have to give myself
the Heimlich again

Will you watch me
like an experiment
as I throw myself
on our dining room set

sit impassive across from me
breathing gristled sage
chewing
resentment
and sausage
and biscuit?

The Saddest Country Song You Ever Wrote

To be performed with gentle fingerpicking on ukulele.

On the way to your memorial

I threw away the pieces of wall
you hit instead of me

The crowbar I kept under the bed
was in the trunk
and I was breathing louder
than you would have liked

We were a love poem once

On the way to your memorial
we stopped to get food
They didn't have the BBQ chips you liked
Is this how I would make you angry again?

Your memorial
was held at the dream home
you spoke of on our aimless country drives
I'm told these hermit hills
sapped your depression
the heart attack
that made you a cruel stranger
did not have weight here

You worked the land like it would save your soul
put my letters cards and love poems in a folder
for your sisters to find
kept my picture in your music room
our wedding songs on playlists

told everyone you loved me
that I never deserved your anger
found their forgiveness for the years
spent furrowed   furious

I only ever wanted you to be happy
and here   you were
you were

So now I suckle ice cream like an abandoned child
let our dog on the couch so I'm never alone
dream about falling asleep on the subway
instead of going to shows
Without the force of your hatred and love
I am walking on Mars

Matty my honey
my first true love poem
this is the saddest country song
you ever wrote

Things I Left on the Road

A peppered moth caught in teeth
The chunks of wall you hit instead of me
The ways I lie to myself
The flicked end of a shared smoke

The postcards of where we fell in love
A scream of rubber where I kicked you out
Your apartment keys rusted in the wake of us
A sunburned sloughed-off thumbprint

My deep and varied wombat ways
The box cutter dropped from my boot
A ten-piece band of guys I used to fuck
A bounced bottle of plastic poor choices

The musical saw on a hot Taurus roof
A cowboy ring left in a graffitied
gas station washroom crusted in pink soap
Enough charm to get a room for the night

The body that fell in front of us
The memory of my first pedophile
The cassette tape ribbon unravelling Patsy Cline
The feeling that life could be anything

IV

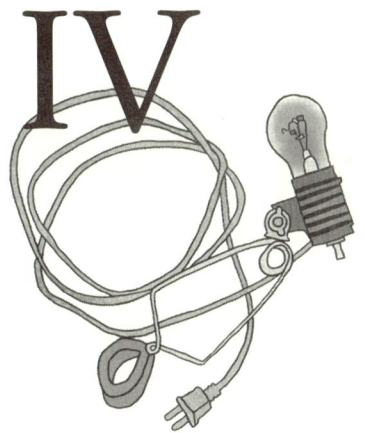

My Body Is a Vessel?

As someone who appears
to have a uterus
I often hear that my body is a vessel

Oh a vessel?
Like a submarine?
Like the Millennium Falcon?
Like a luxury cruise liner?
I imagine tiny umbrellas
little deck chairs
chlorine smells coming
from my splashy-pool belly button

But no
    Tick tick
they say
    Women are having children
    well into their 40s
they say
    There's still time
    to find another husband
they claim

I hear trans couples are adopting
well into their 50s
I hear some women
are not having children
happily into their 90s

My body is not missing anything

    (other than a better spleen
    and some interchangeable sex organs would be nice)

My body is a vessel for art
for unfinished poems
unfinished love affairs
unending affection for whatever family I have

And yes
maybe I did watch *Eraserhead*
a few too many times to truly
enjoy the sounds of a newborn babe

I still go to pageants and hockey games
and recitals and I've read
bedtime stories to kids
I've held as babies
I am proudly Uncle Charlie
and when your child is old enough
I will teach them how to swear
and bring me booze

My body is not a vessel
it's not waiting for a seed
and though many parents will tell me
I am missing the greatest love of all
you need not remind me
of something I will never know
because as a human

I am aware
being childless
can sometimes be the greatest gift
you can give
because kids
need people
who want to be parents

Medical Secretary Phone Etiquette

Your voice
on the phone again
wet rotted leaf slop
through my earpiece

Before I can misdirect you
the tale of your botched colonoscopy
has begun again

the hose flying out
the blockage sloshing
a clump of you
careening away from fecund home

I draw a little gun
firing a bullet
on a Post-It note
hold it to my temple

Your breath sounds so moist
more like a stoma
than lips

The waiting room seems
like a theatre set
I can almost smell
aftermath

and here we are
fused in polite horror
the story now fully drained

Forward & Reverse

The day after
toxic masculinity
turned a Toronto rental van
into an automatic weapon
used to kill women

I was afraid to walk faster
than the man ahead of me
of the men who spilled from
bars to pat my dog
afraid for her when she
didn't want their hands
clawing
helping themselves to her body

    Is it a girl? She looks like a girl
they ask
She looks at me
    Why?
She looks at me
    Run

and because they are each a cocked gun
I say that she is and smile and walk away
aware we are always moving targets
who are only permitted to scowl
in death

The day before
toxic masculinity
turned a Toronto rental van
into an automatic weapon
used to kill women

I was afraid to walk faster
than the man ahead of me
of the men who spilled from
bars to pat my dog
afraid for her when she
didn't want their hands
clawing
helping themselves to her body

    Is it a girl? She looks like a girl
they ask
she looks at me
    Why?
she looks at me
    Run

and because they are each a cocked gun
I say that she is and smile and walk away
aware we are always moving targets
who are only permitted to scowl
in death

Complicated Migraine

A numb tongue
and a left hand
with no feeling
I tried to make jokes with you

though your face was an
upside-down watercolour
I needed to laugh about this

let drool an aphasic plea
that you play
"Candle in the Wind"
at my funeral
even though
it's for blond women

I think it took me
five minutes to get this joke out
Thank you for letting me

What would we do
without laughter?

I didn't panic
I told myself
not to panic

If this was a stroke
it would be the adrenaline
that would kill me

but when they asked me
my phone number
and it became
digits drifting
cursive and coiling
out of reach
I cried

I have so enjoyed
my brain

Days later
the world is shattered glass
stage lights are howling owls
too-fast drumbeats are bar brawls

I push myself to finish this poem
on a backlit screen
My best tools have become tortures

I'll laugh
until my last breath
because
obstacles
are punchlines
in my book of
how the fuck to live on earth

Postictal

I was the thrum throb
the interjector
the three-way
talk tentaclist
the corraller
the cacaphonator

Now I crawl
under tables
of conversation
wonder when
we are all

going to say
nothing

One Year Since Your Death

I remember us
arms across bellies
legs draped over lap
or fitting puzzle-piece
folded good night

Next I feel you in my lungs
the spasms of laughter
the harmonies of songs
breath on cheeks

I hear you in
mandolins strummed
     One more song Matty
backyard nights
how you made us sound like stars
moments of eyes over violas
ballads of
     I love you

When I hear our music
on the radio now
it feels like I'm slipping
down stairs

I don't care about how we broke
how our marriage became a sputtering jalopy
leaking fluid in withered sunshine

It's been a year of going backwards in time
of watching you get further from me
of finding you in the strangest places
of falling in love
with our moments
when we were in love

La Visite

Inspired by Jean Paul Lemieux's painting La Visite.

Before arriving
at winter dinner parties
let the shame
condense in the car
Permafrost cruelties
trace blurted buckshot words
on windowpane
Be aware that
heat will reveal them again

Show your daughter
how to cool her brow
Take her laugh lines
in both hands
run your thumbs
over her bird-brittle bones
Let nothing
stay written
in her eyes

There is an art in fighting
to win
in living with lichen
in confessionals
built into Buicks

and knowing what to offer
winter dinner parties
Find out the main dish
anticipate what is needed
sweet or savoury
Say nothing of infidelity
or what became of your name
during that long drive
Keep your wrists covered
so no one
can see
how you scream

Muscle Memory

(Sometimes I write single-stanza poems, for example,
the other day I woke up and wrote :)

Don't tell me
I'm strong
ask me how
I got there

(Then for the rest of the day I was worried
someone would ask me how I got there. So I wrote
this next poem :)

How Did You Get to Be So Strong?
Potential Answers

Public transportation
I just stopped showering

I am my own problem

El Caminos are my favourite car
Pro wrestling and Pop-Tarts
Molestation
I knew Snuffleupagus existed and
told no one on Sesame Street

White Jesus looks like
every guy who's raped me
I eat meat and love animals

White supremacy helped me
afford therapy
Doesn't survival
really just mean
alive?

My ex-husband's death
made me a Widex
which sounds like Windex
I can find ways to laugh about this
Thank fuck I can laugh about this

Didn't Bambi make a career out of grief?
I just have good comeback lines

As a child I preferred Band-Aids
to looking at my own skin
I love the smell of gasoline
My breasts don't belong to me
so in a way
some of it didn't happen

I breathe easiest in emergencies
My first best friend is psychotic
Wolves only turn on the weakest
I want to be seen as a man
Isn't this how to be a man?

My brain is actually a maze of
safety deposit boxes

I've been taught
the terrible art
of how to walk tall
on stolen land

I am surrounded by people
who need to be stronger than me

Because artists save me every day
Because my art saves me
Because the stage is never
the only open palm
that holds me up

V

One Year Gender Queer

I wear a costume every day
Sometimes shimmering sequins
or fake fur furrowing fantastic ideas
butchering stuffed animals
for pelts

I used to starve to be gender neutral svelte

a rough angled queen in
boyfriend cut jeans
buttons forever on the wrong side of me

I walk upright in
men's fineries
push my head back over my shoulders
uncoil my neck from when
I ran from my body
physiologically

I have cufflinks for the French shirts
tie clips clipped to my wings
earrings that only last an hour
     Get these off of me
I go from boxer to G-string
         (I'm just kidding about the G-string
         I spend most days
         keeping things from disappearing into
         the wormhole of my ass)

I do work drag
drag to go shopping
drag to sleep drag to eat
drag to think drag to get paid
drag to supper drag to dunch
drag from dawn to dusk
drag to breathe
drag to brush my teeth
everyday is drag to me

Maybe it started
was when I heard
my gender all wrong
and endlessly tried to be
"mistaken"
for a boy
until breasts grew on my body
and puberty
became robbery
I didn't grow up
in an era that could define me

Please bind me
corset me
push me bend me
separate me
cut me bruise me feel me
tell me how to feel
me

because sometimes my skin
is crumpled on your floor
and some days
I want nothing more
than to be muscle and bone naked
because I can't handle the
drag of the day

because she
makes me feel like a man
and he
makes me feel uncertainty
and they
make me feel like home

My Musical Saw

To be performed while playing the "Ave Maria"
by Franz Schubert on the musical saw.

You've been called eerie/haunted/evil
but I hear you nightingale

You are a string strung
from my neck to my knee

I am the body of my instrument
every movement pitched

Each ounce of space
is a note

I shake in time
feet bouncing

knees clamped together
arms pulling pushing bending

Each motion
paints mouths metallic castrati

You let me imagine out loud
bring voice to memory

Ideas are notes
a prayer of thoughts

You're a joke turned on the teller
a miracle of tension

music can come from anything
willing to speak

Passed Tense

*To be performed while playing the viola & singing
saw on a loop pedal.*

Weren't we
the kind of tense
that held bows over stings
strings to necks
chinrest in place?

Remember that time,
you tilted my head up?
That time you told my
jaw to relax just
by holding it in your hand?

You took the musical saw
from between my knees
the bow from my fingers
and I let you
until you left

My music holds these moments
when we were love spent and supine
twines them around
tightens them until
they can sing again
until my body is poised
in the absence of you
and there is no relax
there is only music

horsehair taut over wire
or spine of saw
wishing you could
be here

my mouth and eyes closed
my moving body a sound
of wood and string and steel
an ache of love notes
where your name used to be

Translucency

Swallow the trans button
you have on your jacket
Push the ones from your backpack
under your nails
Set fire to the cotton balls
that ingested the eyeshadow

Would you like us even smaller?

Something that can
be shoved into a drawer
pressed into bible page
What would be more
convenient
transportable
solid   liquid   or gas?

Remember that time
our pronouns made you nervous?
Oh the fear that we'd correct you
Can you hear how silence
is an endless scream

But you could never
remember that new name

Look at all the little boxes
unchecking themselves
being lowered into the earth

There

you can finally
say their old name again

Just Some Band Names I Think Are Cool

*To be performed with super cool garage rock music
that I make with my mouth, a foot tambourine, & a
loop pedal.*

Yer Mom's Hot
Socks Aren't Shoes
The Side Effects

Our Drummer Sucks
The Rigged Awards
I Wanted More for You

Pay for Art
The Spineless Weasels
You Don't Deserve Her

What's That Smell
The Has-Beens
Swedish Fountains Are Fancy

Lapses of Reason
Solid Waste
You've Let Your Father Down

The Angry Hopefuls
Little Accidents
Adult Onset

Stop music

(Okay so this next one probably won't fit on the
marquee but...)

The "We're Going to Come Over to Your House, Break
Your Toilet, Break Your Heart, 'Borrow' Money, Smoke
Your Stash, Call So Many Terrible Things We Do
'Sharing' but Never Repay Any of the Damage We Cause
Because We Think That We Deserve More Than What
We Get and Our Heroes Seem to Be Able to Do Anything
They Want to Fans So We Want to Keep Up That
Tradition Because We Are Afraid to Show Weakness or
Talk About Why We Haven't Written Anything New
and It Is This, Our Self Hatred, That Will Become Your
Downfall and Yeah We Let Your Cat Out By Mistake, Can
We Have That Sandwich You Promised Us"es

I Am the Bat-Them

To be performed while wearing my sleep mask.

Maybe you've seen me
sleep masking between subway stops
I put it on so that the flashing lights
won't steal my ability to walk
to think
to speak

Perhaps you've taken a picture
It's hard for me to tell   whenever
I take the mask off
you're not looking anymore

But I can smell you
sense the pressure of air around you
You forget that I can still hear
you guffaw and wonder aloud

    I am the Bat-them
I think, or
    Daredevil
or anyone more powerful than me in this moment
a disabled trans on transit

Hope that the next time someone
grabs me while blindfolded
they will let go

That it will not be the beginning of an attack
The scenes I play in my head
of what will happen each time I put on the sleep mask
could make wallpaper want to leave the house

I don't expect other passengers to warn me
I have lived in this city too long
to expect heroics   however small
but
at least I don't have to watch you
laugh at me

Beautiful Baby Blank

A poem for Fox.

Your birth name wasn't your choice
It was for the suckling baby
the smooth-skin cherub
the blank-slate bubby
who everyone expected
had been identified

There are only two boxes
on birth certificates

short coffins
of gender
Let's lay you in one
Oh my what a beautiful...
                    (insert echoing heckle here)

Boxes that should be canvases
that ask only to be filled in
with an X
when you could fill it
with a cubist abstract
But you're and F
or an M
Fuck Me

Be an other
Be a hieroglyph
a stick figure myself out
Tell them that little boxes are cages
We are all born free
until the birth certificate shows up
Before it does though...

there is a heaven on earth
where you are loved
as light   as energy
as human

Maybe That's Why You Left Me

My mouth is a trap door
and we both got lost in it
and that's why you left me

My feet are so beautiful
with sandal weather approaching
you were worried
you'd never want to leave me

My voice became
the special ringtone you set for me
but then it irritated you
and I became that ringtone

It wasn't me it was you
It wasn't you it was boo
It wasn't boo it was boo hoo
It wasn't us it was the movie industry
It wasn't the industry it was the outcome
It wasn't the outcome it was capitalism

I was never warm enough for your climate change
You were never cold enough for my climate change
My apocalypse doesn't match your apocalypse

It was faith
the way it is liquid silk
the way it becomes a breeze
We left the window open
on your seventeenth-floor apartment
and it just slipped out
and like my many fake moustaches
I didn't see it on the ground there
and trampled it into my boot cleats
and now it's just a clump
of what we used to be
and maybe that's
why you dumped me

VI

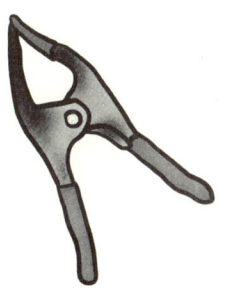

Why Did the Trans Kid Cross the Road?

*In 2019, Ontario's newly elected provincial Conservative
government scheduled a debate about the existence of trans
& non-binary people & gave out a hotline number to report
teachers talking about gender identity or respecting pro-
nouns. Our former Liberal government had made it essential
for schools to welcome trans & non-binary identities.*

1. I am six years old. My identity has no words. The crossing
guard asks me if I'm a boy or a girl. My mouth is a goldfish.
I start to cry. He asks again, and because he sounds mean, I
say, "Girl." I don't know what to do with the feeling that this
is a lie, and I almost throw up from the rush.

2. I imagine this incident as a recent one. Occurring under our
former, more inclusive government. When the crossing guard
asks me if I'm a boy or a girl, I tell him, "I'm transmasculine."
I tell him my pronouns and that my name is Charlie. Maybe
he's still mean, but now, he can't say anything.

3. I imagine I am that kid today. This morning our new
government has instructed schools that trans and non-binary
identities aren't real. I approach the crossing guard. Yesterday
I told him my name and pronouns. Today he is holding them
as a handful of blades. He asks me, "Are you a boy or a girl?"
and I know it's mean. He grips the pronouns, my blood spills
between his fingers. I run. He doesn't stop the cars.

My Neighbour Is Practicing
Biological Warfare

There he is again
reeking of long-ago showers
his hair getting the matted
SPCA smell
picking at the scab
his face has become

Yesterday for no reason at all
I ate my body hair
until I puked

The day before that
it was clam juice
and Captain Crunch

Last Wednesday my ears bled
and I could only walk on four legs
and speak gibberish

I never felt like this
before he moved in

Maybe I should call someone
but every time I lay
cold-sweat hands on the phone
I hear his mouth click
the orifice agape   a swallowing gulch

and I'm inside of it
We both pretend he's not staring at me
taking notes
observing
When I step out of my house he's

clipping clipped-bare hedges
raking nothing in the yard

or standing an inch from the sheer curtain
that barely hides his veiny eyes

Today the stench from next door
is all hopeless tree-sap sweet
and metal gnashings

Slapping tongue sounds
seep through the walls
I want tacos
breaded raccoon droppings
and for my legs
to stop melting

I write about sex/ If I wrote about baking/ would I owe you pie?

After you die
I remember you scribbling
in my teenage notebook
that time we lived in a booze
can and only we knew the way
out and it was a dollar store notebook
your poems always rhymed
and mine had such sharp edges
I think I was bleeding the whole
time and you smiled so sadly at
how my boyfriend would abuse
me in front of you and years later
we met again and I said *Hey I haven't
seen you since the orgy we had*
which is hilarious but then you
were in my house so fast
telling me how your favourite
role onstage was a rapist
and you pretended to lose your shoe
so that I would feel awful about
kicking you out and I made out with
you because you told me you're
not treating the cancer this time and
it wasn't me pitying you that's not it

it was me realizing that there was no fear
left in you and death was pushing you
on me and you said *I write such*
filthy things because I want sex
and later I wrote a haiku about that and
everyone laughed but me and when
you die I mourn only the boy you were
when we dreamed of escape together

Our Love Is Groundless

When you tell me you love me
I orbit the earth

Palliative Care for Problematic People

To be performed while building a sound loop of viola,
ukulele, & a vocal stating the title of the poem, while
grieving onstage.

Witnessing a lion
        become a mouse

is a humbling
surgery

Transilience

Trans is waiting for your name to get called
while the teams go ahead
and play the game on top of you

Genderfluid is the shiny new car
that your parents think is a wreck
and will never let out of the driveway

Non-binary is rehearsing how to exit the bathroom stall
in a way that will get you past the four men
surrounding it
but not incite their violence

Gender non-conforming is running up to cis people
asking
       Is this how you felt in your skin this whole time?
while they stare at your high five until your arm withers

Transmasculine is walking well behind women
so they don't get worried while evading men
who follow you too closely

Fluidity is taking out the pin
from the *How can I help you?* grenade
and hearing the answer click on retail floors

Coming out is revisiting the library in your brain
and closing so many books that had remained open
waiting for answers

Trans is whispering to your child self
      I'm so sorry I didn't listen to you
      Let's give you the life you deserve

Speaking Bradbury

Time held us
between sheets
by lamplight
our anatomy easy
and in love

I opened the covers
of Ray Bradbury
used his words to
paint orbits around your head
trace the body
of The Illustrated Woman

Nothing else in life
would let you fall asleep
with such ease

Though your sister held your hand
as you died
and our wedding ring
has been buried in the backyard
since before you left
and you hadn't heard my voice in years

I hope somehow it returned
Held you past the sundown
that always made you sad

Spoke to you of Mars
melancholy
and all things fantastic
That you somehow knew
how loved you always were

Cows Whisper Murder While Climbing Planks

Nothing good comes of marching
or climbing planks

I've watched my mother
single-file step
bleating beatitudes
of staying meek

> *My daughter*
> *when this happens be still*
> *you want the first bullet to work*

My son
my sweet solace
to this slaughterhouse
they call him
tender
they call him
veal
I call him
my baby

All five of my stomachs
pull knot-taut
at the single barrel shouts of
I'll never see you again
chewed digestion
is never loud enough
to ignore
the last thing
you'll ever hear

One time
farmer got drunk
yelling drunk
kicking stalls drunk
fuck you cows
drunk
and he showed us
his handgun
fired it
into the air

How different it sounds
when it's not landing
in our brains
simple flight
wasted shot

How to Tell If a Poem Is Trans or Not

A helpful guide for slam poetry judges.

Look directly at the crotch
Gently wave away all
thoughts about how
you never cared about crotches of poems
before this poet

Consider the subject

is it about love   loss
surgery   hesitation
breath   death threats
surgery   surgery?

Does it rhyme?

Look at the crotch again

Don't look up to see the poet looking
at you looking at their crotch
there's no need to involve them
in this ruptured universe

Grasp for any gendered word
Is tree bark about being a man?
Are they saying anything about blood
or ribcages? Ribcages are a trans thing now?

Stare at its chest
They're saying
something something
    inclusion now
or was that
    foregone conclusion

Wait don't you have to score the poem?
How can you score it if you don't know

Oh why did they write about a Jack pine
it's all so unfamiliar just words like an apogee
with no point of gender reference

They look trans
why aren't they talking about that then?
Talk about that then

Time's almost up
Their crotch is telling you nothing
Do you score them like a cis person?

Maybe they're straight   dear lord
did you get it all wrong?
How low a score can you give them
if they might not be trans?

They warned you about slam
now here you are

crotchmerized

I'm So Good at Drag

*To be performed with the ukulele, foot tambourine,
thunder tube, musical saw, viola, basically anything
that can make noise. I add these to the loop as the
poem builds. Also features my "cool dad" dance moves.*

I'm so good at drag
I got the doctor to put "female"
on my birth certificate

I'm so good at drag
my parents called me
   Ca-ther-innne

I'm so good at drag
I got the job and over performed
and still didn't get promoted
but I did get sexually harassed
and my ideas stolen

I'm so good at drag
my boy band
tried to pay me less
than the other guys

I'm so good at drag
I'm allowed to cry in public
be excused from manual labour
and can say things like
    I wish I could give birth
and nobody laughs at me

    (No I don't want to give birth   I was just trying
    to make a point)

I'm so good at drag
some of my cis male partners
thought we were having
straight sex the whole time

I'm so good at drag
that some of you
don't understand
what this poem is about

Notes

Previously Published:

"Dear C-3PO" in *CV2*, Vol 43, 2020

"My First Boyfriend" in *Descant*, #163, 2015

"Waltzing Armageddon" in *Descant*, #163, 2015

"Why I Was Late" in *The Malahat Review*, #205, 2019

"Transilience," published & produced as a poetry video by *DailyXtra*, 2018

Acknowledgements

An artist is born but also raised by the communities that surround them, so I say thank you to our poetry communities of both page and stage, specifically to Plasticine Poetry and Toronto Poetry Slam who supported my growth with applause, critique, and action.

I thank my family—you have grown with me so much, and I am always grateful for the love and support I get from each of you. I am a lucky guy.

I thank my chosen family for so often holding me through these moments, for the deep support I've experienced in my transformation, and all of these moments captured in this work of a decade's worth of creation.

Thank you to my film union siblings, to my co-workers in health care. You all do so much with so little and are true punks. Thank you to my book blurbers, Amber Dawn, Kai Cheng Thom, Mary Lambert & bill bisset. You are all so very excellent.

Thank you to Brick Books, to my editors Andrea Thompson and Nick Thran, and to the wonderful artist Emmie Tsumura for the glorious cover. These objects are each so important to me. Artistic credit goes to Niizhokwe(Shaelynn Recollet) for her handsome gift of a birch bark bow tie, featured on the back, and Jimson Bowler for the beautiful handmade ring.

Look my loves, we made a book together.

Charlie Petch (they/them, he/him) is a disabled/queer/trans-masculine multidisciplinary artist who resides in Tkaronto/ Toronto. A poet, playwright, librettist, musician, lighting designer, and host, Petch was the 2017 Poet of Honour for SpeakNorth National Festival of Spoken Word, winner of the League of Canadian Poets' 2020 Sheri-D Wilson Golden Beret Award recognizing lifetime achievement in spoken word, and founder of Hot Damn It's a Queer Slam. Petch is a touring performer, as well as a mentor and workshop facilitator. Find out more at www.charliecpetch.com

Colophon

Why I Was Late was designed by Emmie Tsumura in June 2021, on Treaty 13, Tkaronto/Toronto. It was printed and bound by Coach House Printing.

The typeface used throughout the book is Dante MT, designed by the German-born typographer and master printer Giovanni Mardersteig in the mid-20th century. During WWII, he was known to help political refugees find safety on other continents and published anti-Nazi sonnets through his own press.

The cover was designed in collaboration with the author, using imagery from Charlie's poetry. It explores a tender reflection on masculinity, depicted by a collection of objects floating together relationally in an everchanging space, each carrying their own history and intrinsic value.

The photo included with Charlie's biography was taken by Alessandra Naccarato.